As
Butterflies
Rest

Are you growing through changes?

by **Morgan Paige Shorts**

cover by **Christa FreeHands**

edited by **Carmen M. Hall**

Family & Friends: Thank you for loving me through
my craziest of times.

abandoned attachment
aggravated ashamed
addicted codependency
confusion doubt entitled
blaming being judgemental
being too emotional
  excessive focus on others
extremist, insecurity
forgetful, irresponsible,
living in the past, irritated
materialism overspending
procrastination, people pleasing
pain, self conscious, moodiness,
not seeking approval, unappreciate
uncertain

Larva

I take in all outside of me
To shed all that's on me
To bring forth all that's in me
For purpose to live through me.

Out of Reach

I ain't been feeling right
lately
          I ain't been filled
right.
His reach ain't reached
me.
          I am out of his
reach.
I am deaf to truth.
I am mute to confess.
I am blind to my wrongs.
          I am the living
dead.
I am smiling, depressed.
My room is a mess, dirty
     I, I wait til the last
minute to begin
          I never have time
for nothing.
I hide in deep, dark places
Finding solace in
uncertainties.
              I
give what I do not have
Leaving me in the
negative.
          Damn I want
to be positive.
I love the right people
wrong, leaving me left.

          They left
me.
Here.
I hear you
But,
I'm not listening.
          So here,
            I'm
giving you what you
don't want.
I don't read your
blueprint of why
You feel the way you do
& I disregard every
Bullet point,
Example,
And all suggestions of
how I could do better.

I feel nothing.
So your love ain't
enough.

**You ain't been felt,
right?**

Please Them

If I agree with every thought you possess
I know that we won't go wrong.
I have the thoughts I own
But my need for you to feel comfortable in your own
is more important than my need to express.

If I hang onto every word you say
I can shape shift into whoever you want me to be
it's swift how I people please,
but I have to beg and plead for people to listen to me.

The things you do that bother me, I don't tell you
Because every time I do
it leads us to argue.
My ego is bruised
I got PTSD addressing my problems with you.

Silence begets me.
Internal wars, my conscience vs. my mind
My insides self-destructing in me.
Warring with how I feel and who I want to be to them

I'm Siamese, it's two of us sharing me
Gemini, I lie, I'm two faced
I got two mind's
I'm thinking two ways, too much.

Me vs. Them
No it's Me vs. Us
I understand when I can't, they don't believe me.
Can I blame them?
I don't believe me.

I lie to me.
I'm my enemy
I'm the enemy.
I'm at the end of me

I'm dying to please.
I'm dying of two me's
If I die for them
Who gone live for me?
If I hold me within?
They still gone look outside for me.

So, this is my last attempt at suicide
and the first time that one takes their own life
and still lives.
I didn't die to please them
I had to die to me.
For me.

Identity

Push me to the edge and I won't jump.
I won't fall.
Nor fail.
It would be easy to figure me out if I didn't change so much.
If I didn't grow at the touch of God's hand.
If I didn't know who I was.
If I operated at such a miniscule level, it would be easy to ridicule me.
It would be easy to judge me, if you didn't see what you were saying of me in yourself.
Easy to love me if you loved you.
Easier to accept me if you accepted yourself.
Look in the mirror.
Who are you?
What do you bring to the table?
What are you worth?
What do you want out of life?
What do you like?
Who do you want to be and why?
What do you want?
All of these questions I sit beside myself and ask
Because my identity is important to me
How I feel about myself gets me up each day.
And how they feel about me gone change anyways.
I know myself.

I know how I can be.
I know what it's like to look to other's for clarity.
So I define myself.
Sit inside myself.
Look at my reflection to realign myself.
Mirrored images get the picture but don't see what's inside.
I declare my I Am's in the mirror and I say them with pride.
My professions are a life sentence or a death certificate.
Even if not yet, I Am and I say it until I believe it, tears rolling, my heart might not take to it at first but my subconscious gone receive it.
No need to miseducate.
There's always gone be debates, but it's no question when you're great.
I am Great.

Royalties

Who do you know to make mankind feel like they deserve
us and still know that they don't?
Black Women.
We collectively come in different shapes and sizes
and we can just about pull off anything.
But our natural sets us apart.
All of us, natural, but our natural really can't be mimicked,
it's more of a parody.
It's a rarity to not see a black woman as a mother because
we've been raising other people's kids since back in the day.
And they acknowledge us but not in the way that they
should.
And I guess gradually they'll come to realize we aint they
mamas
but they should honor us for the example we set.
For the strength they forget we gotta carry because
sometimes our black men become blind to us.

Our men scared to look in the mirror and have their asses
handed to them, I guess I'm problematic.
So they'd rather look at the opposite and feel like they doing
opposite and she apologetic because of her ancestors.

Funny,
When a white man calls you beautiful, you look to him like
Jesus.
Because the total opposite of you finds you attractive and in
my head I'm hoping this man don't think I'm attracted.
I was made for a black man.
That's my preference.
And I know we all use this as a reference

I hope that this digests and that you don't take it out of context.

Black women are royalties.

Who you know that could birth a nation with her dna?

This man got a black mama but he looks like he of a different race.

Black women are royalties.

So you'd pay a pretty penny to be us or steal us.

Sell our organs so a white man can have a baby he was never destined to.

Or you'd get lip injections, wear butt pads, fat transfers to acquire bigger assets.

Imitation should be flattering, Nah

Not when it's stealing our identity

Not when it makes us feel like property and at any point we aint got no place, no home, no safety.

We just out here left to roam. Confused as to where we belong.

The only thing they don't take is our voice.

And they figure we aint proper or poised.

So, they ignore our cries, our strife.

Letting us die

Making up lies

Ruling it as a suicide

All over a traffic stop.

Black women are royalties.

Like we owe them

Like calling us pretty for a black girl is a compliment

Like we had control over what we looked like

As if we were afforded the same rights

Or asking if we're mixed with something as if it would make us better.

Black women are royalties.

When we die in hospitals for poor treatment or no treatment

And being misdiagnosed for illnesses we never had

Or our names being mispronounced on purpose
As if this is all that we amount to
If you know how to read my name is Morgan, not Megan
it's simple.
 However, the simple gone ignore the or because I'm more
than just the royalties of this world,
I'm royal.

This Baby

There was no excitement, no anticipation, not even a shared
love. This was unknown, blindness, a secret in my womb.
Hidden. Buried. More than just a dream.
To me, this was necessity.
I knew I'd be overjoyed to be with child.
In a blink. I was over joy when I learned I didn't hold this
baby right.
It's my fault this baby didn't try.
This baby was fragile and short lived.
This baby seen my inner parts had just endured loss.
Different, but of the same magnitude.
There was emptiness there.
This baby was wise. This baby was closer to God than I.
This baby knew it couldn't survive inside my life at this
time.
This is where darkness lives.
Resentment would move in and stay for a while if this baby
resides.
This baby seen a shattered heart.
This baby knew their new home would be torn apart if baby
had tried.
This baby was wise. This baby was closer to God than I.
This baby was an angel. This baby had a message.
This baby showed me my insides wasn't right.
This baby was life.
This baby didn't have to cry for mama to hear him. This
baby was easygoing.
This baby was wise.
This baby was closer to God than I.

Dear Lord, I come to you on behalf of every woman that purchases this book and every woman in relation to the person who has picked up this book. Thank you for your love and mercy. Thank you for your guidance and wisdom. I ask that you reveal and remind us collectively and individually of who we are. Our worth. And whom you have destined us to be, our purpose. Forgive us for our sins Lord, removing any and every feeling of guilt and shame attached to us. Lord help us to let go of our old ways: unhealthy mindsets, poor judgements, past relationships, hurts, rejection, gossiping, fear, codependency. And guide us into a new way of being: free, drama free, light, joy, refreshing, loving, and forgiving. Lord give us a new mindset. Lord help us not to idolize after unhealthy relationships and give us the ability to dream again. Lord I ask that you light a fire in the hearts of women who have given up on themselves and feel that they have nothing to look forward to. Lord I ask that you bless them with ideas and drive to manifest and live out their purpose. I cast out the spirit of fear in women who have ideas but are scared to see them through. Lord deal with our insides. Help us to get to the root of our issues within: depression, anxiety, insecurities, abandonment, gossiping, lying, manipulating, past hurts from family relationships, friendships and partners and guide us to seek counsel, be counseled and healed through your word and professionals instead of just shoving it under

the rug. Lord I ask that you help us take back control of our emotions and show us how to express in a healthy way. Bless and heal the wombs of those who have endured loss through miscarriage or abortion. Lord I ask that the women who have experienced a miscarriage their hearts are healed and restore their faith in being able to carry again. To the women who have experienced an abortion Lord I ask that you heal their wombs and heart and if desired, they'll be able to carry and birth a beautiful baby. Lord align our desires with your will. I hope this prayer doesn't fall on deaf ears. I believe you will bless these women on every border of their lives: Spiritually, Mentally, Physically, Emotionally, & Financially. Lord, **your will** be done.
In Jesus name, Amen.

My grandma went on to be with the Lord and all I can think about as a believer is how we long for this moment. The moment she met. My grandma made it! My grandma made the devil tremble. She woke up and went to sleep praying. She's went to God on all of my family and my friend's behalf. My mom, grandma, and godmother have been on the other end of the line of most if not all of my breakdowns and what they all 3 had in common was 2 Corinthians 10:5. I think the most beautiful gesture is having someone go to God about you, for you, with you. My grandma did whatever she could for her family. She took me in when I was rebellious and spoke so much life into me. She always pointed me to the Lord. A woman who devoted her life to sharing the good news. A precious gift, when someone would share the same hope that they have for themselves, with you. It would be selfish of me to say it wasn't her time, I want my grandma back, or something else taking this moment from her. I will miss her, her cakes, her prayers, her subtle "love checks", her food; her presence. But 2 Corinthians 5:8. This is her moment.

Bev Interlude

We gone get deep
like undertones
Tissue
Bones
Flesh
That's what has you acting like that
Like you ain't got no damn sense
Since your grandma then left.
You see eyes nose that you can't deal with all
the emotion from you losing your senses.
Her physical presence made sense.
A pillar that if removed everything else came
crumbling down.
She was monumental.
I ain't never felt loss this deep they say,
"man you mental."
How you think?
What you think, when cancer hits?
Stifling her very being.
Your face's sake.
I cry puddles of grief til my face aches.
Cancer is so cold.
It affects everybody that person touched like he wants
to get a hold on her and rip the soul out of us.
It don't feel right.
My flesh eating me alive,

It's a cancer in me
Like my birthday in the middle of July.
Raging empty,
I'm trying to feel something or nothing
at all
"my grandma is gone"
My soul mourning the whole morning I knew she left
before I even got a call.
She was leaving when I landed.
God set it up so smooth, he knew I had to be on the
other side of the country.
He knew I would've drove to our home that we shared
for a little
and stayed there for years on end.
On some, "No!"
Ya'll not moving her body I want her to lay there.
To watch her rest was a rarity.
I thought cancer took her ability to walk.
But I feel now that God said it was time for her to sit
down.
It was time for her good deeds to be returned to her.
She did so much for so many.
It was time we serve her, pray for her, pray with her.
Cook and clean for her.
So she sat,
First the natural then the spiritual
because God was getting her throne ready.
So she sat and she laid, while we glorified her.

Beverly

Sometimes I feel numb and other times I'm filled with
deep sentiments.
Extremities, I'm learning to cope with.
Physically, I miss you.
Spiritually, I know you remain a dwelling space inside
time.
An era of love, I abide in our moments.
I often travel the realms of my memory to experience
you again.
The echoes of your intercession still having moving
power in this dimension,
is a testament there is no way to measure one's
ascension.
You made brick homes in minds and hearts that if hell
met me there,
the foundation you built remains unscathed.
What is physical has ceased.
Yet, your love transcends touch, depth, & time.
There is no line to divide or subtract your influence on
my existence.
You've multiplied my destiny through your transition.
And at conversion your seat was planted at the right
hand of God.

Dear Lord,

I come to you today just a little under or down trying to figure some things out. I'm just confused. I'm not sure if this confusion came once I let ████████ back in or not but I need clarity. Lord please forgive me for my sins. Help me to see and hear from you Lord. Lord get me out of this spell. I rebuke anything or anyone that keeps me from you Lord. Lord please forgive me for my sins. Have mercy on me like the lper. Jesus touch me. Lord deliver me from my insecurities. Lord help me to love all people as you love them. Help me to see people as you see them. Lord please give me the strength to go on w/ my days. Lord excelerate the process. Lord take my dependa on ████████ away. Lord I want to rely on you. I trust you Lord. I believe in you and I want to see your works. I want to see what you have in store for me. Lord your will will be done. Lord I have faith I will be delivered. I will make 100% effort. Thank you for your mind + mace than you

STUCK

I've written this text with different year sequences 10
times and still I stay.
When the lesson hasn't been learned you get stuck.
And I wonder, "I must like to suffer."
You don't understand me.
And I conform to being misunderstood.
You never get what I'm saying.
You're stuck in your own beliefs.
What do you believe to be true about me?
Do you even know what I want?
Do you know who I want to be?
Do I even know what I want?
I'm stuck here.
Trying to please you, something I never do.
Us both,
stuck.
I guess neither one of us have the balls to say,
"it's time for me to leave you."
Instead it's, leave us alone.
Us against the world we made that up.
As if the world was against us.
However, the way the cards were dealt you never had a
Queen. And I never had a King.
Just two Jokers looking to mean something to
somebody.
You were my spades partner.

Somehow, we could never read each other's hand
so we'd cancel each other out with who we are:
two jokers, looking to mean something to somebody.
Sure, we meant something to one another.
What is definition to someone who could never
define you?
Since this is love,
us - being stuck.
Is this all that we amount to?
Card games, text messages, and questions
that leave you questioning, if we're just stupid or
through all that we've been through our relationship is
destined?
Except there's no progression.
So stuck,
is us
in our element.

September 5th, 2018 1:00am

Nothing settles w/ me. I'm not
secure in your this relationship
im holding on to. I'm not getting
anything I want. Nothing heart
felt. Nothing serious. Nothing
firm enough to stand on. I cant
compare I cant look down upon.
Never could, im getting the same
if not worse For years I come
around and at the end of the
day, no title. I could say on I
know what we have between us
but what do we have? The door
is left open for me to not be
disappointed yet be hurt if
something was to happen. Lord I
see how things not built on
you - how cloudy, how
wrong they are. We'll try
to mask it. Be blind by it.
it's cloudy yet so <u>clear</u> when
I do want to see it or hear

Hollow Hearts

I learned my lesson with the last tear that slid
down my cheek.
I knew love didn't feel like that
wasn't supposed to.
He was wasting my good love.
He didn't feel it.
Numb to my touch.
Wouldn't drown in my deep.
It was too much to comprehend.
He couldn't understand how I so freely loved him,
Certainly.
No boundaries.
He didn't deserve me.
Still, he deserved that love.
20+ years of heartache
He earned a beak.
My love fed his ego.
Yet,
It never eased his pain.
How do you patch up a heart when the right
atrium is missing?
Left atrium still pumping
I put my head to his chest
To check, give his heart a listen
Step back, look at him, dead in the eyes
How is he still breathing but dead inside?

My love didn't stand a chance
I thought that my love could move him
How?
When he's paralyzed.
Maybe my words could transform his mood.
He read into everything I didn't say.
He was deaf to peace.
He was dead to me.
I tried breathing life back into him
There were holes all over.
Inflation was impossible.
I was rooted in planting new life on bad soil
I was determined to uproot my life
To help get his in order.
My love was sacrificial.
I'd do anything to make him feel better
I'd hate me along with him just to be on the same side.
I hate me, with him
That wasn't a façade.
Maybe I love him because I'm scared to be alone?
I fear me without him.
Who am I without him?

AWARE

- I am aware that in regards to the color of my skin I am judged more harshly than those of other races.

- I am also aware that we've been living in times that by the color of my skin I place fear in the heart of those who don't relate to me in that manner.

I honestly don't know how much more aware I can be.
I sit and ponder on how there's no justice in the land of the free.
And how a man loses endorsements just for taking a knee, receiving death threats kneeling for what he believes.

- I am aware that if a man decides to take advantage of me, I was asking for it.

Raping me is not a disgrace to thee.
Your leniency in Brock Turner's indecency
I declare there's no justice in the land of the free!

Six months in jail that's all he gets?

Three years' probation is proportionate?
- to a lifetime of regret in going to a party with
  my sis?

- how uncomfortable I'd be with a friend of the
  opposite sex?

- my disbelief in the justice system who validates
  my rape because of my unconsciousness?

Six months is all he gets?

• At this point my awareness of certain matters
  has surpassed my ability to think logically.

So right now,
I'm analyzing every Black Man shot on camera.
Somehow, I feel that the news, government, & police
department are provoking me.
Enlighten me on how we are supposed to react to live
video of a Black Man being shot?

Repeated daily,
Shots are fatal
No chance of reviving his life.
His legacy is fabricated with a hashtag and a story line
to justify he was a threat to society and no longer
needed here on earth.

• More aware now than ever that the Black Man
   has been a target since birth.

Somehow you used your white power and
convinced our ancestors that we were a product to
be owned, bought, and sold.

Contrary to popular belief, our African ancestors sat on
a throne.

So, I just can't be a modern day slave.
Be silent, sit back, and mourn.
Sit quiet, dwell, scorned.
Watch you kill another Black Man and form
yet another case,
justifying the massacre of another black face.

Here, For You

I know you use to people counting favors
They take back what they gave to you
List all the things you've done wrong,
call you names and they blame you.
For all the problems they go through, "because of
you."

Let's be clear: I'm here, for you.

We both know what I've done for you, there's no need
to discuss.
I'd never take it back, it was done out of love
If it makes you feel alright to say you gone pay me
back, cool.
But I'm not taking notes on what I've done for you.

Understand: I'm here, for you.

If you do me wrong and we come face to face
I won't spew fire at you or throw dirt on your name
I'll look you in the eye and with a hug of forgiveness,
we'll embrace.
The love we share remains

Never forget: I'm here, for you.

I'm here,

for you.

I was called to you to show you love is action.
Love is not measured by how many I love yous
and then they're retracted.
I ask you questions because I want to understand you
I support you in your choices, I'm not here to
reprimand you.
Any advice that I give is only an investment to the
betterment of you.
I want to see you doing better than what you thought or
believed before.
I'm speaking life into you.
I'm into finding solutions.
Not adding problems leaving you to solve 'em

I'm not here because you do this
or if you do that
ima do this

I'm here, for you

For Colored Men

I watch you
Matter of fact,
I gaze in admiration of your strength
You carry the weight of hate on your shoulders

Despite it all,
You glow
Fluorescent gold,
   Bronze,
       Black,
           Chocolate,
              Opal,
                  Mocha,
                    Caramel
I'm aroused by your drive.

The way you maneuver through this life
It's like you got power..
Steering, day to day
Resilient to say the upmost.

Your stance is head strong
Like this world is trying to
Suck the life right out of you.
But you take it, dead on
You ain't afraid to die.

These other races, well you know
But no fear, you're here.

They want to take you out when they sense you
coming.

You are powerful.
And I'm not just talking physical.
We know that, they do too.
I'm talking demeanor
You exude authority,
Like a king,
         Master,
                 Your highness.
You got that quiet, cocky
A confidence, I speak highly of.
Yea, never accept nothing less.

It may sound like I'm praising you
And I am.
I'm speaking to the god in you.
Master your I Am's
Tell me who you are, you are Him.
Whatever you say after, I Am.

I feel a mass amount of empathy towards the black man in these times. You see day in and day out how a black man can live up to and meet the highest standards that society sets and still a black man will be seen as a criminal, a thug, and or deemed negatively. I admire the strength and resilience of black men throughout our country and beyond. I respect the nature and the essence of black men as a whole. I see you. I respect you. I honor you. Dear Lord, I come to you on behalf of every black man that has picked up this book, and every man that is in relation to a woman who has purchased this book. Lord I ask that you protect, lead, and guide these men as they walk about this earth. Lord, I ask that you open their minds, hearts, and hands to receive this prayer. Lord I ask that you reveal their purpose to them and fill their minds with ideas, knowledge, and understanding to walk their purpose out. Lord on behalf of these men I ask for your forgiveness, I ask that you remove any shame, guilt, or negative feelings they have of themselves. Lord I ask that you help them to see the royalty they truly are and to take on the identity of who you have created them to be individually and collectively as Black Men. Lord give them an "I Am" testimony and show them how to use their mouths to declare their identity in you and who you've called them to be. Lord, I believe if it's in your will all will be done. In Jesus name, Amen.

I can't wait to know you
~~and~~ meet you, you seem too
good to be true.

04-23-2013

My heart murmurs for you.
~~my~~ every thought is surrounded
by my want and need for you.
I ~~need~~ pray you survive in me.
It scares me to know that my
stress could be the cause of
your harm.
only to know that you are a product
of me and your father.
the strength of my love for
you noone will ever understand
        to know you, just to
be in your presence.
I love you ~~need you~~ with every
cell, chromosome, atom of me.
my soul yearns for your heart.
beat. I need you to survive
just to hear your heart beat
... only to hear your little
        heart beat.

An Ode to Ava

I've written about you since before you were born.
But, I didn't know you yet, only what I hoped you be.
I thought my love for you had reached capacity
I learned there's no cap on my love for thee
And my cup runneth over with glory to God that
He felt I was worthy enough to be your mother.

I refer to you as my star
Not only because I know I'm raising someone
important
But since I've given birth to you,
You lit up my life
put the sparkle back in my eyes
I understand, why I never considered abortion.

Your strong will challenges me
Although I want to give you everything
that you want.
I don't want you to get confused
in regards to our bond,
I'm not your friend. I'm your mom.

Disciplining you is hard for me.
As I watch you harbor your tears
I want you to understand
I only discipline you – to teach you obedience

Always remember it is your shield.

There's been times I wanted to give up
Down & out,
Contemplated taking my life.
Although I have friends, family, purpose
It is you who has kept me alive.

Our bond, our constellation
Is more than what meets the eye.
Greater than an opinion,
Only outsiders can provide
How you reciprocate your love for me?
Ma, Are you okay, Are you alright?
At only 3 you were consoling me.
I'm not only blessed to have you here with me
But to have carried you inside.

I have promises to you that I plan to keep.
There are understandings we'll always have
Through our eyes, no need for a speech.
You get me.
So many questions I had of my existence,
And you are the answer.
I know there are lessons planted in you
That as you mature they'll sprout.
God is teaching me through you.
Simultaneously as he's teaching you through me.

We are in divine assignment with one another.
You are an extension of the greatness that I am.
I see you **greater than, higher than**
what any man or friend will convince you to believe.
You are worth more than gold.
There is nothing or no one you can be compared to.
You are unpredictable.
You are filled with infinite possibilities, gifts, and powers.
You are a spirit, a light, a feeling that can't be compromised.
You are confident, strong and mighty.
You are honest, kind, and a woman of integrity.
You are soft, beautiful, and intelligent.
I honor and respect your decisions.
Your opinion matters to me.
I'll answer all your questions.
Yet, I hope you never question me.
Unless your only question is,
What wouldn't my mother do for me?

An ode to **Aua*** (10·27·16)

I've written about you before you
    were born
~~and now that know you~~
    but I didnt know you, yet
    only what I'd hope you be.
My love for you has reached capacity
and my ~~every~~ cup runneth over
    with Glry to God
        that He felt I was ~~worthy enough~~
to be your mother.

I refer gto you as my star
not only b/c I know ~~your~~ I'm raising someone
~~they someone famous~~ important
~~mom~~ also since I've given birth
to you, you lit up my life
        put the sparkle back in my eyes
and ~~now I know~~ why I never
        understand
            considered abortion.

You strong-will challenges me
~~much~~ although I want to
    give you everything that you w

A

Golden brown girl
eyes to match,
You have your father's smile
and your mother's soft.
Sassy and you know what you want.
I love that about you.
You just are.
Always inquiring about things beyond your years
I wonder if you've been here before.
Your dreams seem prophetic
You speak like you know something beyond
elementary
Like you graduated in another dimension that I wasn't
there for.
God has His hands on you.
I know that, I just prayed to be a good steward
and guidance on how to grow through life with you.
Your heart is art handcrafted by God
Sufficiently precise, you are a product of love.
Who am I to doubt His hand? His work?
Who would I be without you?
Barren,
I'd imagine
Mind, Body, and Spirit.
Without you I'd be a lost cause,
looking to find you in iniquities.

What's destiny without purpose?
You are purposed for my destiny.
This life that I create revolves around my stewardship.
You are at the hand of God
I'm just who He partnered you with.

01-27-14

    Today marks 3 months of Ava's existence. Thankyou Lord for blessing me with a beautiful daughter. A healthy daughter, a pleasure to raise her. Lord please equip me with the traits and qualities to raise her to be the best that she can be. Lord please help me to stand my ground with Gerald, help me to stay focused and not let my emotions ruin my life. Lord I know that emotions are temporary. Help me not to react off of my emotions. Lord please become the center of my life. Help me to make every decision based off of your liking. Lord help me to be less

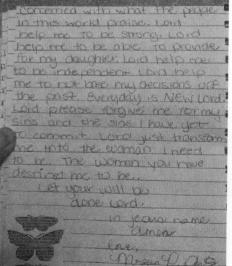

concerned with what the people in this world praise. Lord help me to be strong. Lord help me to be able to provide for my daughter. Lord help me to be independent. Lord help me to not base my decisions off the past. Everyday is NEW Lord. Lord please forgive me for my sins and the sins I have yet to commit. Lord just transform me into the woman I need to be. The woman you have destined me to be..

    Let your will be done Lord.

        In Jesus' name
        Amen

    love,
    Morgan D. Chate

Dear Ava,

I love you so much. You are almost 1 week old and I could not be prouder to be apart of your life. To raise you is the biggest blessing God could've ever granted me with. Holding you, feeding you, changing your diaper... I cherish all of those things. You are so strong to be so little and I admire you. You motivate me to keep pushing, to pull through. You are my strength. God has you here early for a reason. You are a force to be wreckoned with. You are loved by everyone. And I hope you remember this. I promise to show you I love you, every second, minute, hour of the day. You are my one and only. My beautiful Ava Ca'ryn I simply adore you.

love,
Mommy 11/1/2013

Lord reveal secrets unknown to me. Help me to come to grips with reality. Help me to see the importance of my actions. Lord I declare today that I will make money. Money blows to me exceedingly + abundantly out of the hands of men. Lord I am beautiful, joyous, hopeful, kind, virtuous, respectful, worthy, forgiven, loved, compassionate healthy all because of you. Lord for allowing me to have many I AM's. Lord but 1st I Am your daughter + I want our relationship to reflect that.
In Jesus Name
Amen
Megan Paige

...between...
I can carry out your will. Hoping to find a baby sitter for Ava tonight. In Jesus Name I pray Amen

8·18·2018
thankyou Lord for a great work day, great tippers, great people. Lord thankyou for your love and your word being taught through men + women around the nation. Thankyou for my gifts you've blessed me w/ that are known + unknown

Scriptual

I gift chills often through regular conversations
My presence is often longed for
My dialogue lifts weights off the heaviest of hearts.
I understand why men would want to grace me with
titles such as bride or wife.
I am the bride to Christ.
I resonate with title well.
As I am an author made in the likeness of my father
who art in heaven.
I am like Him. I am His child. I am His. I am God's
I am.
I am spirit. I am one with the holy trinity. I am one. I
am at one.
I know my beginnings and how I'll end is in the power
of my tongue.
I am sacred.
And it's scary.
It's hot in that church and I got cold feet.
Sacred and scared are the same word when you switch
the ac.
and the switch up is what leaves my soul aching.
I am fearfully and wonderfully made.
I fear nothing or no one.
Except The One who created me.
I am.
I am creation. I am creator and creative

I am.

I am bible like stories. I am words. I am bond.
I am bonded by stories.
And the word was with God, and the word was God.
I am.
I am home. I am abode.
My body is a temple of the Holy Spirit who is in me,
whom I have from God, and that I am not my own.
I am church.
I am.
I am seen. I am meteor.
There once was darkness now I see. I am light.
I am.
I am loved. Eternally. Unconditionally. In spite of.
I am love. I am whole. I am complete in him.
Apart from him I can do nothing.
Apart from him I can't do
Apart from him **I can't** is part of my vocabulary
Apart from him I
Apart from him there's no I
Apart from him
Apart from
Apart.
Apartheids. Parts tides. Down the middle. Feels
lukewarm
Like which side you gone be on?
Like whose guy is this?

I don't belong. Like who am I?
Like I'm confused?
Like nonchalant. Like ignorant
As if no one understands.
My plans? There are no plans.
Like separated from. Like Divorce. Like Flesh.
Like babies out of wedlock. Like lockdown.
Like bound.
Like I am,
Without Him.

Dear Lord,   12·15·14

Thank you for today. Thank you for waking me up this morning. Please forgive me for my sins Lord. Lord please bless me with overwhelming peace of mind and peace in my spirit. Lord help me to be a better woman, mother and friend. Help me to practice new routines and help me to take control and responsibility of my actions and emotions. Lord help me to love like you love and get my goals that I set accomplished. Help me to not get so caught up and moved by temporary emotions and feelings and thoughts and people but to be moved by permanent, consistency

Love is not love until you love in spite of.

Once I heard this quote it immediately moved me to open my bible to 1 Corinthians 13 4-8. This scripture describes love to its fullest extent. Love is not just an emotion, its action. Putting away your pride to simply say I love you does not suffice as a means of fulfilling the action of love to someone.

I am loving you by extending and practicing patience and kindness with you. I am loving you by not boasting about my love for you but freely giving you my love and not trying to make anyone envious or jealous of my love that I am giving because it is a gift I give to anyone/ everyone. I am loving you by not keeping record of your wrongs and not allowing your wrongs or sins to influence me to form a bad judgement or the wrong impression of who you are and how God sees you. I am loving you **in spite of** your wrongs, your sins, the things that you do that influence me to feel some kind of way. God has loved me **in spite of.**

In spite of all the dirt that I have done. God loves me in spite of all the lessons he has taught me even when I decided to go my own way. God has loved me in spite of my disobedience.

Can you think of anyone, including God who has loved you **in spite of?**

I am loving you by not giving up on you, by being hopeful and enduring the hard times as well as the good times with you. I am loving you not because of what you do for me but because God loves me **in spite of,** I ought to love everyone I encounter **in spite of**. Although my loving **in spite of** will never amount to

Love Acknowledged

Window seat. And I see the world as wide, as grand, as detailed as God made it. As if science could formulate this masterpiece of humanity. As if this just existed before time with no founding, no creator. A maze of wilderness beneath me. Who could fathom this? And bring it about into fruition. Fruit trees providing nutrition to beasts unknown and Adam calling them by name. Whatever he came up with. And to think I was gifted with that same power! Me? **Powerful.** I see clouds. Fluffed like pillows beneath the right wing of this aircraft. My God, the works of his hand so vast to be confined to this bible. This book. Yet and still I read because I don't want to be confused as to who it is when God speaks to me. I need to know His voice. His tone. He sounds like a man who loves me. Not a human love. This love is in spite of me. This love has nothing to do with me. He sounds like a grandma who would tear your butt up if she heard you talking like that. He sounds like a police officer, that's going to let you slide this one time for speeding. But, the next time…you won't get off that easy. He sounds like a pastor hitting what you're going through right on the head, resonating well within you. He sounds like a mother there to comfort you, reassuring you with a soft word that everything will be okay. As if she knows something you don't.

He sounds like a friend, a friend that reminds you of your worth. There, to join you with a good, hearty laugh when ya'll look back on the things ya'll did in the past.

My creator, who gave me one of the most powerful machines known to man. My brain. A mind, to create these beautiful masterpieces it stretches wide to get a glimpse of who He is and still can't capture the full picture. I'd imagine him to look like an intergenerational, multicultural family photo stemming from existence to present day. He looks different and the same all in one. I see glimpses of Him in everyone I meet. That's why I love. This love resides in me, uncontrolled, immense, continued. This love has nothing to do with me.

And everything to do with Him.

Psalms 139:16-17

Your eyes saw my substance, being yet unformed.
And in Your book they all were written,
The days fashioned for me,
When as yet there were none of them.

How precious also are Your thoughts to me, O God!
How great is the sum of them!

(it just sounds so poetic and lovey-dovey to me)

In our mother's womb we were formed and He had a plan
for us even before then. A unique plan for each and every
one of us. Our whole lives mapped out in our mother's
womb. And that is why I pray His Will and His Way. Every
time I ventured from His will and His way things never
went well or only went well for a little bit. God's way is
perfect. His will was designed with you in mind. Things
above anything you could ever imagine. He had BIG
PLANS for you in your mother's womb. He had your
husband/ your wife picked out in your mother's womb. He
had your career set out for you in your mother's womb, the
gifts, and the talents instilled in you in your mother's womb.
That is insane. To know that God thinks of me. He thinks
highly of me. Not only me but you too. David says, "How
great is the sum of them!" He thinks about you all the time.
How heartwarming is it to know that God - the same God
who created the earth, the moon and the stars - thinks about
you? My God thinks about me, a lot. No matter what, He
thinks of me. He doesn't forget about me. It only goes to
show how big God is - we all are on His mind. How does
God keep up with every individual plan for each and every
one of our lives? I'll never know.

Own It

1-888-474-3587, the number I called to find
somewhere to go
Never imagined I'd be in the position of not having a
home
And dialing that number in a kitchen where I ate.
The same kitchen whose owner asked me to come
there in the first place.
The phone rings and they answer, directing me to
refuge.
Unbeknownst to myself those were my directions to
find you. Me.
And my child, she's smiling as I'm trying to hide my
tears.
Never in a million decades did I fathom taking her to a
shelter. In this moment I was a failure of a mom.
But, this was my first coming and her first home was in
me and wherever I was
So, I guess I had to get comfortable living within my
own, as she did.
Overcome by hate and shame as I drive to this place,
I prayed to Love for peace.
Known for losing my cool, this prayer was a cry for
warmth.
Love replied with heat.

Walking through those doors, I was at ease forgetting
where I thought I was going.
I can't remember faces or exact words it was late
But, I remember I had all my senses.
My heart contracting on the brink to give birth
Seeing how clean smelling this sanctuary was
I realized I was in the pews as we entered our room
Standing before the bed I laid on the alter
Purpose infecting me as if the bed was anointed or
something.
I went to sleep that night and dreamed.
My perception of happiness and my future died in me
that night.
Those feelings of hate and shame were tricks of the
enemy.
This moment was meant to be.
A baptism in it's own sense.
And since then I haven't wanted for anything more
from that day forward but to meet the need of those
who met a moment like mine.
I found a home in homelessness.
I found purpose in what seemed like failure.
And when I called, God answered me.

Dear Lord,

Thankyou for this day. Thankyou for strength. Please forgive me for my sins. Lord thankyou for clarity, wholeness, and security. Lord continue to watch over my family and friends. Lord let your will be done. Lord please change my life in ways unimaginable. Prepare me for your will Lord. Change in me what is not like you. Promote independence in myself. Lord I cast every worry upon you. Lord I trust your work. Make me new in you. Cleanse my mind body and soul. Help me to see life in a new light Lord. Help me to be a blessing unto all of those I come into contact with. Lord help me to be a better friend, family member, sister, mother, woman all around. Lord I want to be a life changer. I want to inspire those who are uninspired. Help me to bring people closer to you. Help me Lord to find a place and be a provider. I'm dedicated to you Lord. No weapon formed against me shall prosper. You can DO ALL THINGS!

Amen
love
woman

Pupa

I've taken in all that I can hold
All that I am is a product of my environments
And I would like to die to these moments
Rest In Peace to all of this wisdom I've acquired
And bring all of which I have learned into my
transition.

Air Maxx

You are a breath of unburdened air.
Refreshing to me.
It's easy to feel,
　　To lie in,
　　　　　To breathe you.
Inhale, exhale you.
Just to share you.
With no intent to be possessive of you.
I pass out balloons with remnants of you.
I want to experience you in fullness
and behold the depths of you til no end.
In parallel watching you create,
manifests creation in me.
Formed and inspired by what you produce,
what I deliver is a continuation of
Everything that could be
Us
The sum of uninhibited breeze.
Easy, gentle,
Unconfined.
We
Flow fluently
Harmonizing
You compliment my highs
Beyond a mic
Your mellow tone

Keeps me balanced.
Still I fall just to

Float
       In you.

Honeymoon

I imagine a cabana. Nude drapes, hanging in every direction. Hiding our bodies from everyone but us. My beloved lies there slumbering in the midst of sunrise and gentle waves brushing against the shore. I delight in his soundness. Fixed on the air moving through his body as he breathes. His masculinity displayed in how he rests and not only his stance. Tranquility and power seeping through his pores, beholding me. I bask in a moment that I'll hold onto beyond the days we exist. This, is a moment that brands my bones. I gather myself, arising from where we lay, parting the drapes to allow light in. His eyes meet mine as my back faces the sun. A language we have established long before today and forever more as we arise each morning.
This is understanding.
I am naked before him, Unabashedly. As this is a first in this view. He's seen me naked before, as I've undressed every fear, doubt, insecurity and secret that has resided in the crevices of my being. A nude that only he has experienced.
This is acceptance.

His eyes haven't left mine yet. While I crawl back into bed there is a commonality between us that was once unknown. We share the same space. We became one the night before. Standing in the presence of each other and others reflecting on our everythings. My views have changed as I've experienced this moment: I saw his spirit, reflective of mine, forgiven.

This was purification.

Baptism. Our vows were prayers, declarations, a manifestation of what is to come of us. I, a new woman before God and man, given a new name and identity.

This is regeneration.

I take on my new duties, welcome them, knowing who this is for. This is it. This moment. More than just mom, dad, and the kids.

This is purpose.

Where generations will be born. My life is not my own and my choices are not just for me anymore.

This is responsibility and sacrifice.

Where foundations are laid and traditions are founded. Where the laws are established and love is grounded. Where pride is buried and humility is sound.

This is commitment.

All the moments after I do holds the answers to questions we had. Where our answers are tested upon. What is forever to you?

Can you look past our current circumstances and dream with me?

Images from our first encounters rush my mind along with my initial thoughts of you. I want to remember every yesterday of you. I know you like you've never been a stranger before. And with every second that passes us by I'm eager to learn you more.

Are you willing to grow through changes with me?

Untitled:
(inspired by Motion Picture: Queen & Slim)

Your imagination not big enough for me
Black boy you forgot how to dream
My dreams massive
I could dream for you.
I'd dream for you
Give you something to look up to
Close your eyes to my tone
Lay your head in my lap and let me caress your waves
with a song
I'd sing a song for you, with my fingertips along your
collarbone I'd dream for you.
As big as Texas I'll build a home with this song for
you.
Can you hear it?
Big porch with rocking chairs to match. Porch swing
swaying with the summer breeze. We watch from the
window as our kids run, flip after each other.
Can you see it?
Me, still loving you with this dream
Would you believe me if I said I believe in these
things?
Every time my eyes catch yours it's as if it's our last
gaze
Can you feel it?
This feeling that dreams don't exist without you boy.

I dream for you. My dreams for you are bigger than us.
Because our kids our proof. Legacy with your last
name on it, You see what dreams will do?
A love amongst all the strength it took to get to this
place, be in this space with you.
Imagine us not breathing the same air each day, if our
eyes locking wasn't the same, if close wasn't routine
for us:
Could you imagine that?
I don't want to grasp any other concept than what we
have. So, I won't ask.
My dreams are proof. That I am in alignment with
destiny. Because my dreams came true, when I
dreamed for you.

As Butterflies Rest

On my shoulders,
They say don't pick up anything you can't
afford to carry.

On my hands,
Don't make a mess of what you aren't willing
to clean up.

On my lips,
Stay silent for they won't hear you otherwise.

So I lie there,
aware that my time to emerge is near.

As butterflies rest.

Acknowledgements

First and foremost, I would like to thank God. Thank you, Lord, for creating me. Thank you for blessing me with passion and feelings. Thank you, Lord, for the experiences that have shaped and molded me into the woman I am today. Lord thank you for blessing me with understanding and wisdom. Lord I honor you for your unfailing grace and mercy throughout the tosses and turns of my choices in life. Thank you for my creative gifts. Thank you for keeping me. Your love and thoughts for me can't be measured or counted, I bask in knowing that you're always chasing after me. Which reminds me of all you've done and protected me from. I sit in repentance, knowing you've forgiven me. I forgive myself and search for all the ways to be pleasing to you. Thank you

My parents, James Shorts and Carmen Hall. I honor you both. Thank you for raising me, teaching me and instilling in me the importance of self by being yourselves. Thank you for parenting me the best way you knew how and providing for me. Thank you for not hiding your lives from me and allowing me to live and learn from your experiences. Thank you for allowing me to be a kid and make my own mistakes. Thank you for being honest with me and showing me how to express myself. I am a product of you both and I honor that. Thank you, dad, for showing me what an entrepreneur looks like, taking me on my first dates and being a provider. Thank you, mom, for being an example of a great wife and mother. The spirit of peace you have that rests on you I hope I inherit because you know I'm a little different lol. My work ethic, my goofiness, my temper, my ability to love hard and do for others I get from you, Dad. My creativeness, my regalness, my style, my open mind I get from you, Mom. You two created a genius. Give yourselves a round of applause. I love you both.

To my Pastors, Pastor Mike & Lori Peterson, I just want to thank you both for being used by God. The impact you both have had on my life through your teachings in the most monumental time of my life has truly changed me. Through your teachings, your lifestyle, and your mindsets you have blessed the generations that will come from me. Everything that I have learned from you both sticks to me like glue and I pray that I never forget it. Thank you, Pastor Mike, for teaching me about my subconscious mind, true wealth, and prosperity. Thank you for being my spiritual father. Thank you, Pastor Lori, for being an example of a great wife, an excellent mother, style maven, and entrepreneur.

Siggs, Thank you for your encouragement, your push and pull with my gifts. Thank you for challenging me. Most importantly thank you for being my friend. If I hadn't met you this book probably wouldn't have come as soon as it has. And I'll never forget what you helped bring out of me.

Made in the USA
Columbia, SC
19 February 2023

12684160R00048